IMAGES
of America

PROVIDENCE'S
BENEFIT STREET

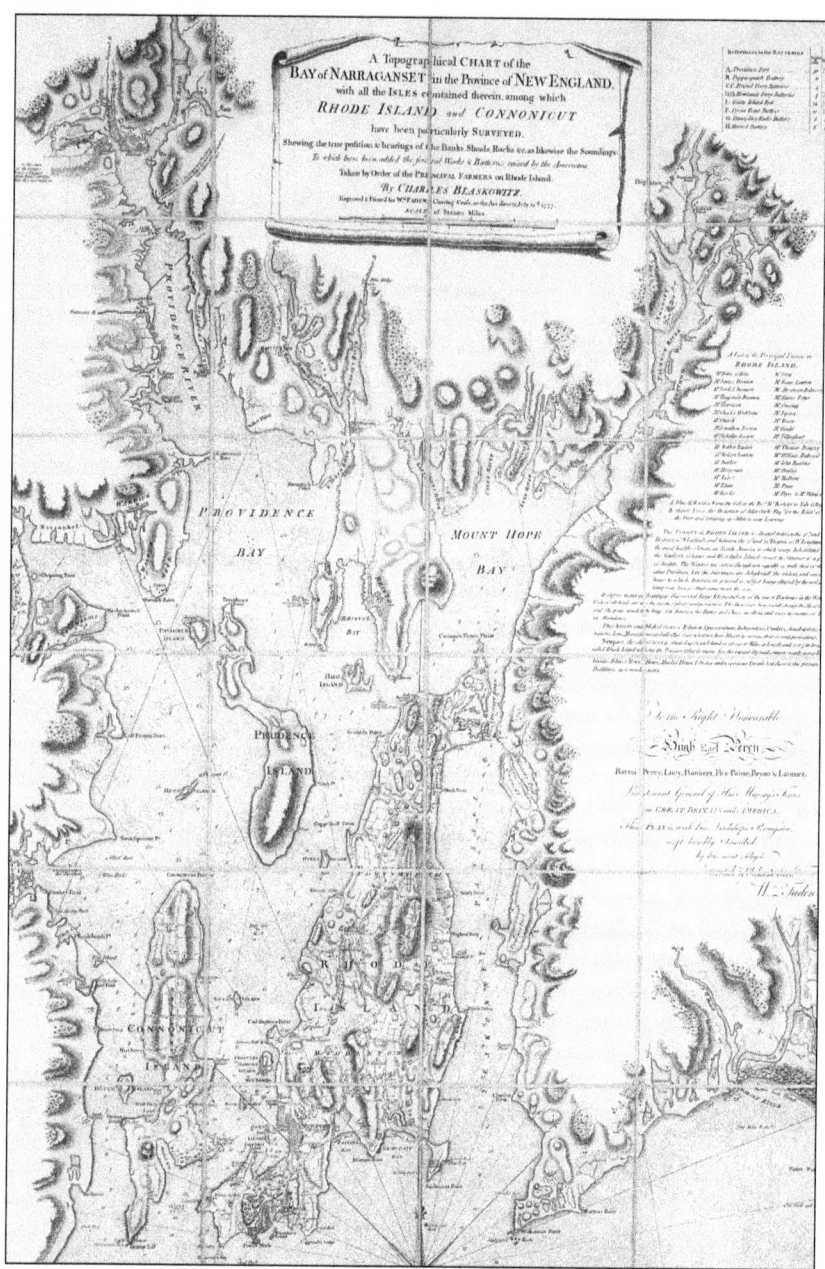

This topographical chart of Rhode Island, by cartographer Charles Blaskowitz (1743–1823), was engraved and published by William Faden (1749–1836) in 1777. The chart shows various large farms across Rhode Island. Benefit Street appears in the top left corner of the map. (Courtesy of the Rhode Island Historical Society.)

ON THE COVER: This c. 1895 image shows the establishment of William H. Cowen, a cigar dealer, one block west of Benefit Street at the corner of North Main and Steeple Streets. Many businesses lined the streets below Benefit Street during the turn of the 20th century. (Courtesy of the Rhode Island Historical Society.)

IMAGES
of America

Providence's Benefit Street

Elyssa Tardif and Peggy Chang
for the Rhode Island Historical Society

ARCADIA
PUBLISHING

Copyright © 2013 by Elyssa Tardif and Peggy Chang for the Rhode Island Historical Society
ISBN 9781531667139

Published by Arcadia Publishing
Charleston, South Carolina

Library of Congress Control Number: 2012953973

For all general information, please contact Arcadia Publishing:
Telephone 843-853-2070
Fax 843-853-0044
E-mail sales@arcadiapublishing.com
For customer service and orders:
Toll-Free 1-888-313-2665

Visit us on the Internet at www.arcadiapublishing.com

To those throughout the centuries who have traversed this "mile of history."

Contents

Acknowledgments		6
Introduction		7
1.	The Early Years	9
2.	"Soul Liberty" for All	17
3.	Merchants and Maritime Pursuits	31
4.	"A Liberal Education"	49
5.	A Haven for Artists	59
6.	Benefit Street in Wartime	71
7.	Taking a Stand	83
8.	Benefit Street South	91
9.	Mile of History, Mile of Memories	109

ACKNOWLEDGMENTS

We are indebted to many people who generously gave their time to assist in this project. Dr. Morgan Grefe, executive director at the Rhode Island Historical Society, encouraged the project from its conception. J.D. Kay, rights and reproductions extraordinaire at the Rhode Island Historical Society, worked tirelessly to collect and process our images. Dr. Rebecca More, Dr. Anne Valk, Dr. Stanley Lemons, Lou Costa, Phoebe S. Bean, Sarah Zurier, and Ed Hooks provided crucial insight and support. We are grateful to Katie McAlpin at Arcadia Publishing for her consistent, cheerful guidance. The work on this project was in part inspired by Mildred Nichols and Goodwill Industries RI, and their interest in the Irrepressible Society, from which they trace their founding.

A thousand thanks from E.T. are due to Barbara Barnes, tourism services manager at the Rhode Island Historical Society. Barbara is an incomparable expert on Benefit Street, a thoroughfare that she loves dearly and that she honors with her excellent walking tours. P.C. would like to thank Tai and Lina Chang and Scott Horton.

Finally, heartfelt thanks to Karen Tardif, Cassandra Tardif, and Stefan Kaszycki for their generosity and limitless patience.

All images appear courtesy of the Rhode Island Historical Society.

Introduction

Providence is a city steeped in history. Evidence of this rich history appears nearly everywhere you look, from the 19th-century facades on Westminster Street to the marbled halls of the statehouse, constructed c. 1901. Even the street signs bear witness to people and structures that have come and gone. Power Street, once Power's Lane, runs the property line of early Providence resident Nicholas Power. Meeting Street was once known as Gaol Lane, where one of Providence's early jails was once located. Transit and Planet Streets commemorate the observation of the transit of Venus, which took place in Providence in 1769.

Benefit Street's name, too, holds layers of meaning and underscores its past importance to the Providence community. Formerly known as Back Street, it ran along the back of many residences, parallel to what was then known as Towne Street. Benefit Street was carved out between 1756 and 1758 for, as the town would later explain, "the common benefit of all." Officially known by 1772 as Benefit Street, the thoroughfare saw houses spring up quickly as certain residents seized the opportunity to build higher on the ridge while still remaining within their property limits. This was possible because of the very narrow, but long, plots that Roger Williams established after 1636, following his banishment from the Massachusetts Bay Colony. In the 17th century, family plots began at the water's edge and extended up the hill; residences were built closer to the water, and the hillside was used for the planting of fruit orchards.

Although the town center began in the early 1700s at the site that now encompasses the Roger Williams National Memorial, the heart of the town ultimately moved south and west, with the Great Salt River and Salt Cove as crucial central points. While Providence was primarily a planting community in the 17th century, maritime commerce would begin to emerge as a way by which some individuals, like John Brown, whose mansion sits along Benefit Street at 52 Power Street, became very wealthy. Earlier in the 18th century, most Providence residents lived on the east side of Towne Street, with the wharves and warehouses used by merchants along the waterfront. At the close of the 18th century, Benefit Street saw the new construction of houses by wealthier residents, and a new surveying of Benefit Street necessitated the removal of most family burial plots to make way for the thoroughfare. With the 19th century, institutions like the Providence Athenaeum and the Rhode Island School of Design were formed, as Providence men and women worked toward creating an artistic and literary stronghold along Benefit Street. The 20th century saw an influx of immigrants to Rhode Island, and the Benefit Street neighborhood followed this trend, as families from Portugal, Cape Verde, and Ireland settled in the south end known as Fox Point. Thus, Benefit Street can be seen as a microcosm of Rhode Island, home to individuals of different professions, faiths, and socioeconomic statuses, all bound together geographically.

It would be impossible to tell the story of Benefit Street without telling that of its sister streets, including North Main, South Main, and Wickenden Streets. While historically Benefit Street has been the location of residences, houses of worship, and educational institutions, these sites would not exist without the businesses that lined North Main Street or the wharves that marked

South Water Street. These streets paint a fuller, richer picture of the nexus that Benefit Street formed in the heart of Providence.

Although this book begins chronologically in the first chapter, the following chapters are organized by theme, emphasizing the variety of communities and personalities that have left their mark on Benefit Street. Chapter one looks at Providence in the 17th and 18th centuries, beginning before Benefit Street came into being and ending just as it was carved out from the ridge formerly known as the "Whatcheer Uplands." (The term "What Cheer" refers to the legend surrounding the founding of Providence by Roger Williams in 1636. After his banishment from the Massachusetts Bay Colony, Williams traveled to present-day East Providence, but upon discovering that it fell under the jurisdiction of the Plymouth Colony, he made his way to the west side of the Seekonk River, where a group of Narragansetts met him with "What cheer, netop?" *What cheer* is the 17th-century version of "What's up?" and *netop* is the word for "friend.") Chapter two, Soul Liberty, explores some of the various faith communities whose houses of worship line Benefit Street. Soul Liberty refers to the notion of liberty of conscience, promoted by men like Roger Williams, which allowed Baptists, Quakers, Jews, and other faiths to worship safely in Rhode Island. Chapter three looks to the Providence River and the wharves and docks that lined it as crucial to Providence's growth as a port city. Chapter four considers the various institutions of learning on and around Benefit Street, and chapter five demonstrates the many literary and artistic figures who left their mark. Chapter six looks to the ways that Benefit Street and its residents experienced war, beginning in the 18th century and ending in the 20th, while chapter seven looks at Benefit Street residents who fought for peace and other such pursuits. Chapter eight explores the eponymous section below College Street that has been home throughout the last two centuries to merchants, middle-class business owners, and factory workers. Focusing primarily on the 20th century, chapter eight shares images of the Portuguese, Cape Verdean, and Irish immigrants who settled in neighborhoods like Fox Point. Finally, chapter nine offers a virtual walking tour of Benefit Street in the 19th and early 20th centuries.

We are afforded these glimpses into the past because photographers like Frank Warren Marshall, John Hess, and Charlotte Estey took it upon themselves to document the beauty of their surroundings, a street that so many have called home for more than two centuries.

One
EARLY YEARS

Alvan Fisher (1792–1863) painted *Providence from Across the Cove* in 1819 from the perspective of Smith Hill. The Great Salt Cove, as it was known, was fed by waters from the Moshassuck River from the north and the Woonasquatucket River from the west. Adjacent to the cove was a freshwater spring, which was the area on which Roger Williams decided to settle.

Peter Frederick Rothermel (1817–1895) painted this portrait of Roger Williams (1603–1683) about 1850. It depicts Williams after his banishment from the Massachusetts Bay Colony. Despite repeated warnings from Puritan authorities in that colony to refrain from spreading "diverse, new, and dangerous opinions," Williams continued to do so. Ultimately, the general court ordered his banishment from the colony; because it was winter, they allowed him to stay for the time being if he did not cause further trouble. Williams still defied the authorities, and, receiving word that he would be detained by a sheriff, Williams left Salem, Massachusetts, in January 1636. Williams made his way first to present-day East Providence, where he was told that the land was part of the Plymouth Bay Colony; learning this, he made his way across the Seekonk River to present-day Providence.

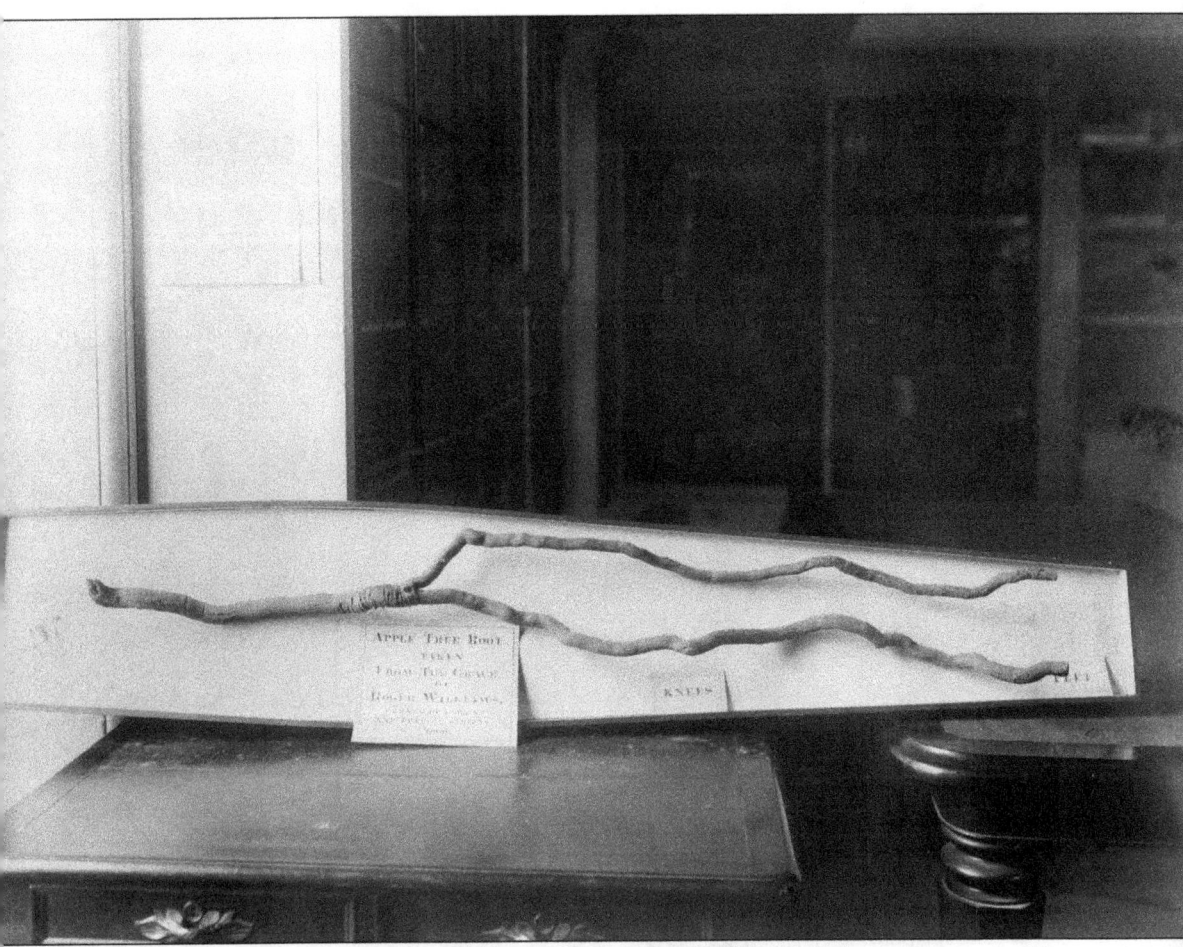

Roger Williams, founder of Rhode Island, died in 1683 and was buried on his own property. The Sullivan Dorr Mansion later replaced Williams's original home at the corner of Benefit and Bowen Streets. According to legend, a group of Williams's descendants attempted to move his body to a new burial ground in 1860. In the space where Williams was supposed to have been buried, the group found a root from a nearby apple tree shaped like a human body. Some claimed that this root actually formed around Williams's body, but this remains a matter of myth and controversy. Remaining bone fragments were transferred to the North Burial Ground where they stayed until 1939, when they were interred in the Roger Williams Memorial on Congdon Street. The famous apple tree root is currently on view at the Rhode Island Historical Society's John Brown House Museum.

This 1909 image shows the purported gravesite of Roger Williams behind the Sullivan Dorr Mansion at 109 Benefit Street, on the corner of Bowen and Pratt Streets. The reverse of the photograph reads, "Photograph was taken by Mr. Willis Andrew Dean, art photographer, Room 15, third floor, Board of Trade Building at Market Square in Providence on Monday afternoon, February 22, 1909." Despite the fact that much has been documented concerning Williams's burial place and the apple root that "ate Roger Williams," there is no extant contemporary description of what Williams looked like. Interest in preserving Roger Williams's records began in the 18th century, and the 19th century saw the formation of the Roger Williams Family Association, open to descendants of the Providence founder.

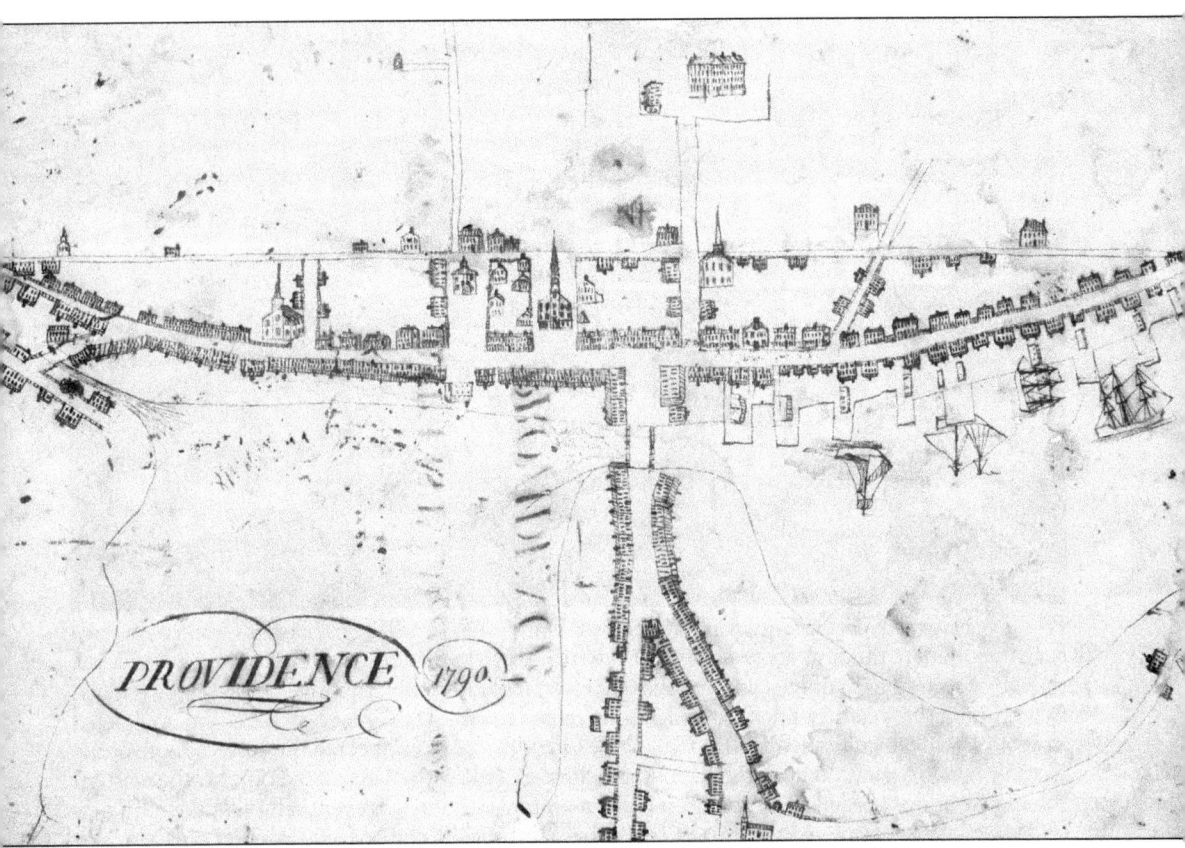

This ink on paper map of Providence was hand-drawn in 1790 by John Fitch, a student at the College of Rhode Island, renamed Brown University. The map depicts houses on Westminster, Weybosset, and North and South Main Streets. Benefit Street is also visible, lined by only a handful of structures in 1790, including the First Congregational Church (later the First Unitarian Church) as well as the John Brown House at the corner of Benefit Street and Power's Lane (later known as Power Street). On the reverse side of the map, Fitch also drew a sketch of the First Baptist Church, the congregation founded by Roger Williams in 1638. At the time Fitch was a student at the College of Rhode Island, founded in 1764, the institution had been located in Providence for two decades. Before that, it was situated in Warren, Rhode Island.

Providence from Across the Cove was painted by Alvan Fisher in 1818. Providence's waterways have been important to the city's economy since it was still a town in the 17th and 18th centuries. Residents, though, struggled to maintain control over the river, including constructing bridges sturdy enough to withstand the weather. The first bridge constructed to cross the Great Salt River was completed in 1660, costing town residents £160. Called the Great Bridge, it connected the eastern shore of the Neck (where Roger Williams and his followers first settled) with Weybosset Point on the western shore. The bridge needed constant upkeep and maintenance and was eventually abandoned; a new bridge would not be erected there until 1711. This painting and the one similar to it on page 9, also done by Alvan Fisher, currently hang on the second floor of the John Brown House Museum.

This drawing of the village of Providence in 1762 shows dwellings along the Neck (in the foreground of the image), the Weybosset, or Great Bridge, as well as dwellings on Weybosset Point. Ships can be seen in wharves along the shore, presumably bringing goods to the Providence port, which would be stored in warehouses. It would take another 10 years, however, for the people of Providence to erect a market house for the sale of these wares. The cornerstone of the Market House was laid in 1773, and the funds for its construction were gathered by a lottery system. The perspective of this drawing looks out onto the Cove from Gaol Lane (later renamed Meeting Street). According to John Hutchins Cady, architectural historian, the drawing was made by Henry A. Barker for a production of *In Colony Times*, a play put on by Brown University during its sesquicentennial in 1914.

This image of the Market House was taken between 1844 and 1849. Residences that line Benefit Street can be seen in the background of the image. The Market House was envisioned for the town several years before they finally decided to move forward with the project. A petition was signed by residents of the town, and a lottery was drawn to raise the funds for its construction as well as for leveling off the ground on the site. The plans for the structure were drawn up by Joseph Brown (one of the four prominent Brown brothers) in collaboration with Stephen Hopkins. John Brown and Moses Brown had helped to fund the project, and Nicholas Brown laid the building's cornerstone in June 1773. The building saw many uses, including the first Masonic hall in Rhode Island (beginning in 1797 when a third story was added).

The daguerreotype above shows the Old Town House in 1850; below is a painting of the same building by George W. Harris, commissioned by Henry C. Whitaker about 1860. Built in 1795 on the corner of College and Benefit Streets, this second structure replaced an earlier one erected in 1723. The earlier building was used as the Congregational church until the new meetinghouse was built, also along Benefit Street. After the church took up a new residence, the building became known as the Town House, hosting the offices of public officials. The Old Town House was demolished in 1860.

Two

"Soul Liberty" for All

The First Baptist Church in America developed an early connection with Brown University, as the university had just moved to Providence from Warren, Rhode Island, five years prior to the establishment of the congregation's third building in 1775. Despite Brown University's break from its founding Baptist ties in the 1930s, this meetinghouse has been used "for the publick worship of the Almighty God" and also for Brown's commencement to this day.

This ink-on-paper engraving by S. Hill, completed in 1789, depicts a southwest view of the First Baptist Church. Although this structure was not completed until 1774, the congregation began to gather in 1638. According to John Hutchins Cady, architectural historian, an area on Mill Street, just west of Benefit Street, served as a "civic center" of the town in the 17th century. The civic center boasted a gristmill, constructed in 1646 and operated by John Smith, that also served as the site for civic activities of the town like the "grinding of the Corne of the Town." The gristmill also served as a meetinghouse, where residents would gather for religious services.

John Fitch, a student at the College of Rhode Island, drew this image of the First Baptist Church on the reverse side of his map of Providence in 1790. The meetinghouse that stands today is the third structure built by the church, constructed between 1774 and 1775.

This view of the Old Stone Bank and South Main Street was probably taken from the roof of the Hospital Trust Building, which is now the Rhode Island School of Design (RISD) Library. Taken by Laurence Tilley in 1952, this perspective also shows the steeple of the First Unitarian Church. Originally known as the First Congregational Church, the wooden structure built on this site in 1795 burned in 1814. The current building, pictured here, was built in 1816.

A prominent stone clock tower rises above the vestibule of the First Unitarian Church, with a wooden steeple reaching 200 feet high. This photograph was taken c. 1910 from the perspective of George Street. The bell featured in the First Unitarian Church is the largest ever cast by the foundry of Paul Revere and Son.

The First Baptist Church in America commemorated its 150th anniversary of the completion of its building on May 21, 1925. The congregation had no meetinghouse until 1700, when the pastor, Pardon Tillinghast, erected a small building on a 20-foot-by-20-foot lot he owned on North Main Street. The rapidly growing congregation necessitated the construction of a second meetinghouse adjacent to the first. Providence's continued growth in the 18th century and the Great Awakening of the 1740s contributed to an increase in the number of Baptists in the city. Finally, the present meetinghouse was built in 1775 and came under the leadership of James Manning.

James Manning (1738–1791), a Baptist minister, was sent by the Philadelphia Baptist Association to work to establish the College of Rhode Island (later Brown University) in Warren, Rhode Island. The college moved to Providence in 1770; Manning served as its president as well as the minister at the First Baptist Church from 1771 to 1791.

The Reverend Dr. Enos Hitchcock (1744–1803) served as a chaplain during the American Revolutionary War. He was a proponent of education, along with James Manning and Moses Brown, and a member of the Benevolent Congregational Society. This portrait of Hitchcock was completed in 1775 and is attributed to William Blodgett.

Joseph Partridge (1792–c. 1832) painted this watercolor image of the First Baptist Meeting House and adjoining buildings in 1822. Born in England, Partridge lived in Rhode Island during the last decade of his life. He advertised himself as a miniaturist who could make portraits of living subjects as well as dead ones. Partridge is known for his paintings of Providence streets as well as his portraits of Stephen Gano and Moses Brown. Partridge seems to have struggled financially, as town records indicate that in 1824, he was ordered to leave Rhode Island as he and his family were destitute. Because he was not a natively born Rhode Islander, the town of Providence was not legally bound to offer support to him or his family. Thus, like other individuals with little or no income in the 18th and 19th century, Partridge was sent out or, more specifically, "warned out" of Rhode Island.

This c. 1818 silk-on-linen embroidery by Sarah Foster Sweet depicts the First Congregational Church in Providence on Benefit Street that was "destroyed by fire June 14th, 1814." Embroidery projects, similar to this one by Sarah Sweet, were taught to young women, girls, and boys in Providence at Mary "Polly" Balch's school, adjacent to Benefit Street. The school was begun sometime before 1785 (the earliest sampler attributed to the school dates to March of that year). The school was started by Sarah Balch, and she and her daughter Mary ran it during its early years. Mary quickly took over the operations of the academy. Samplers were a way by which young people could demonstrate their embroidery skill. These embroideries often include the artisan's name, as well as his or her age at the time of its completion.

Completed in 1816, the First Unitarian Church is one of only two surviving churches built in Providence by John Holden Greene. This is the third building of the congregation, which succeeds Providence's First Congregational Church. The first and second Meeting Houses were erected in 1723 and 1795, respectively. The existing First Unitarian Church replaced the earlier wooden structure that was destroyed by a fire in 1814, when a man suffering from mental illness put a lit candle inside one of the exterior columns. At that time, Providence had little to offer in the way of mental health services, despite the fact that Roger Williams had encouraged the creation of a space to accommodate those "bereft of their senses." In 1844, however, activist and educator Dorothea Dix convinced the wealthy Cyrus Butler to fund the creation of Butler Hospital for the Insane.

For many years, this was known as the First Congregational Church. In the early 1800s, under Dr. Edes, the church became Unitarian and associated with the Unitarian movement in the country. It was not until April 1953, however, that the congregation voted to change the name to the First Unitarian Church of Providence. Changes also occurred in the church's lineage of organs. William Goodrich apparently rebuilt the fire-damaged John Geib organ for installation in 1816 after the second church burnt down; soon after, in 1848, a new organ in a case designed by Thomas A. Tefft was installed in the west balcony. This is a George Hutchings organ, installed in the current meetinghouse in 1893.

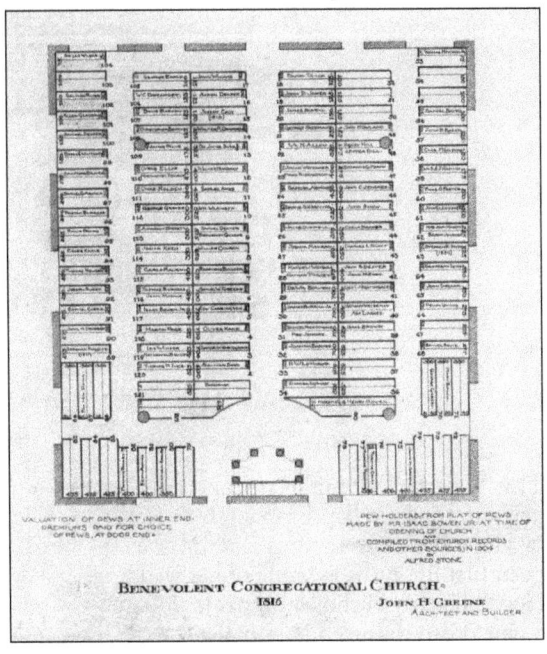

This illustration details the interior of the First Unitarian Church. Architect John Holden Greene chose pew No. 75 for his own because, as Dr. Augustus Lord says in *An Old New England Meeting House*, "from that point of view he could see at a glance the length and breadth and height of the building, every detail of which he had wrought with loving care."

Arnold Block, an 1853 building at 48–54 North Main Street, was owned by James Arnold. Since its establishment, the Arnold Block was home to various businesses and offices, including a medical library, the Fifth National Bank, and Alpha Delta Pi, the Brown fraternity of John D. Rockefeller Jr. In the year before its destruction, it housed the Providence Franklin Society, a cotton firm, and electricians, among others. When the Arnold Block was demolished in 1912, the extension of Waterman Street, now known as Washington Street, was carved between North Main Street and Canal Street. The spire of the First Baptist Church visible in the background rises to a height of 185 feet.

This Waterford Crystal chandelier was given to the First Baptist Church in 1792 by Hope Brown Ives and is said to have been first lit on the evening of her wedding. Hope's brother Nicholas Brown Jr. donated a pipe organ to the church in 1834.

The Women's College at Brown University first welcomed students in October 1891, and enrollment for the first day of classes consisted of six students. On the second floor of the University Grammar School, the women were taught French, Greek, mathematics, and Latin. In the second term, the classes were moved to the State Normal School on Benefit Street.

This photograph by John Hess, a reporter for the *Providence Journal* in the early 20th century, shows the house at 294 Benefit Street as it looked on July 10, 1919. This plot was also used as the site of a Mormon church. The various faiths represented in the houses of worship that make up the Benefit Street neighborhood reflect the principles that were promoted at the outset of Providence's founding. Roger Williams and his followers were adamant that individuals should not be persecuted for their religious beliefs but should possess a liberty of conscience. This did not suggest that Williams himself was an atheist. In fact, the contrary was true, as Williams moved from congregation to congregation, never feeling satisfied with the state of worship he found. Yet, he felt strongly that, although they were likely wrong, individuals with differing beliefs could live in a colony that did not press them into following one particular set of tenets. (Photograph by John Hess.)

This c. 1950 photograph shows the Congdon Street Baptist Church's Youth Fellowship Tea. The Congdon Street Baptist Church was founded on March 9, 1819. At that time, a group of African Americans living in Providence, as well as some whites who were interested in the cause, gathered in the First Baptist Meeting House to discuss the possibility of forming a congregation for the purposes of worship as well as to offer secular education for children in the African American community. A plot of land at the corner of Meeting and Congdon Streets, one block east of Benefit Street, was purchased by Moses Brown, a longtime abolitionist. With funds from Moses Brown, a meetinghouse was constructed, and the building began to offer services in 1821 under the name the African Union Meeting House. This photograph is part of the Congdon Street Baptist Church Collection that was donated to the Rhode Island Historical Society in 1995. (Photograph by Martin Taber.)

These photographs also form part of the Congdon Street Baptist Church Collection at the Rhode Island Historical Society. The c. 1955 photograph above depicts a group of church members. From left to right are Hattie Dudley, Anna Blackmon, Eva Allen, Mary Johnson, and Ed Allen. The c. 1963 photograph below shows an unidentified member standing in her kitchen. Anna M. Blackmon, born in 1879 in South Carolina, was married to John E. Blackmon, five years her senior. At the time this image was taken, the Blackmons were not living near the Congdon Street Baptist Church but 20 blocks away. (Photographs by Martin Taber.)

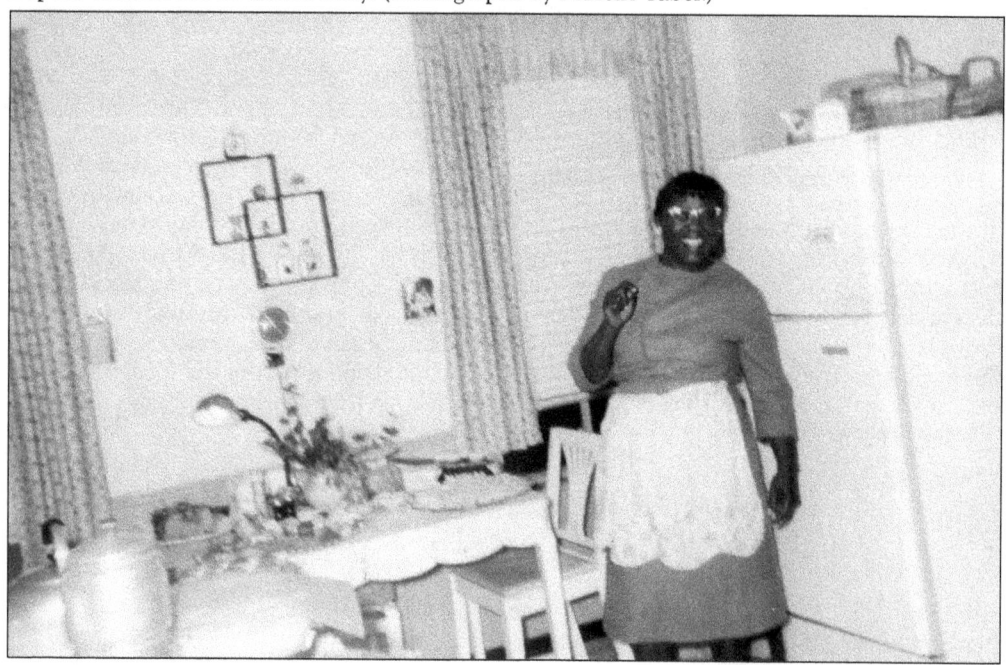

Three
MERCHANTS AND MARITIME PURSUITS

The Fox Point Hurricane Barrier is pictured on November 12, 1962, under construction. The 3,000-foot-long barrier was constructed between 1960 and 1966 to prevent storm surges and flooding in the low-lying areas of Providence. Historically, flooding has been a significant problem for Providence. The hurricane of 1938 that killed 250 people throughout New England submerged Providence under water causing extensive, costly damage.

John Brown (1736–1803), a prominent Providence merchant, commissioned this brick mansion to be built on the corner of Benefit Street at 52 Power Street. Brown sent members of his family throughout the colonies to visit grand houses and asked them to record the measurements of these luxurious spaces so that he could achieve a similar level of quality. Brown accumulated his wealth by participating in the China trade as well as in the slave trade. The voyage of the *Sally*, which he financed with this three brothers, Moses, Joseph, and Nicholas, was particularly disastrous in loss of life and, of concern to John Brown, loss of capital. His brother Moses Brown was so appalled by the death toll of slaves on that voyage that he vowed never to participate in the slave trade again. Moses became a staunch abolitionist, sparring with his brother John about John's continued participation in the slave trade. John Brown's house is pictured about 1965. (Photograph by Laurence Tilley.)

Construction began on John Brown's brick mansion on Benefit Street in 1786; it was completed in 1788. In the same year, John Brown's daughter Abigail married John Francis of Philadelphia at this house when it was still mostly unfurnished. The empty rooms on the second floor were used for a lively wedding reception, filled with dancing and a rousing round of Blind Man's Bluff. This c. 1884 photograph shows the southern side of the house along Power Street.

The John Brown House was given to the Rhode Island Historical Society in 1942 by John Nicholas Brown, a descendant of Nicholas Brown. At that time, the society had been located in the cabinet building, now a part of Brown University. John Nicholas Brown never lived in the house, but he left his mark on it: in the room that Marsden Perry had transformed into his formal dining room, John Nicholas Brown installed a set of wallpaper panels that told the story of Washington's inauguration in New York City. The wallpaper was designed and drawn by Nancy McClelland, considered the first American female interior designer. The panels were each painted individually by artists as part of a Work Progress Administration project. Only a few of these wallpaper sets still exist.

When Marsden Jasael Perry (1850–1935) moved into the John Brown House in 1902, it had been home to the Gammell family for several decades. Perry made many changes to the exterior and interior of the property. For example, he lined many of the walls with hand-painted leather wallpaper, installed what would become a world-renowned Shakespearean library in the basement, and adorned the ceilings with Colonial Revival reliefs. One of the most visible changes that he made was to raze a house on his property on the corner of Charlesfield and Benefit Streets. The house had belonged to Robert Hale Ives Gammell and was bequeathed to his daughter Elizabeth Gammell along with the John Brown House. It is unclear why Perry decided to demolish a house in very good condition, but it is possible that it obscured the view that he desired.

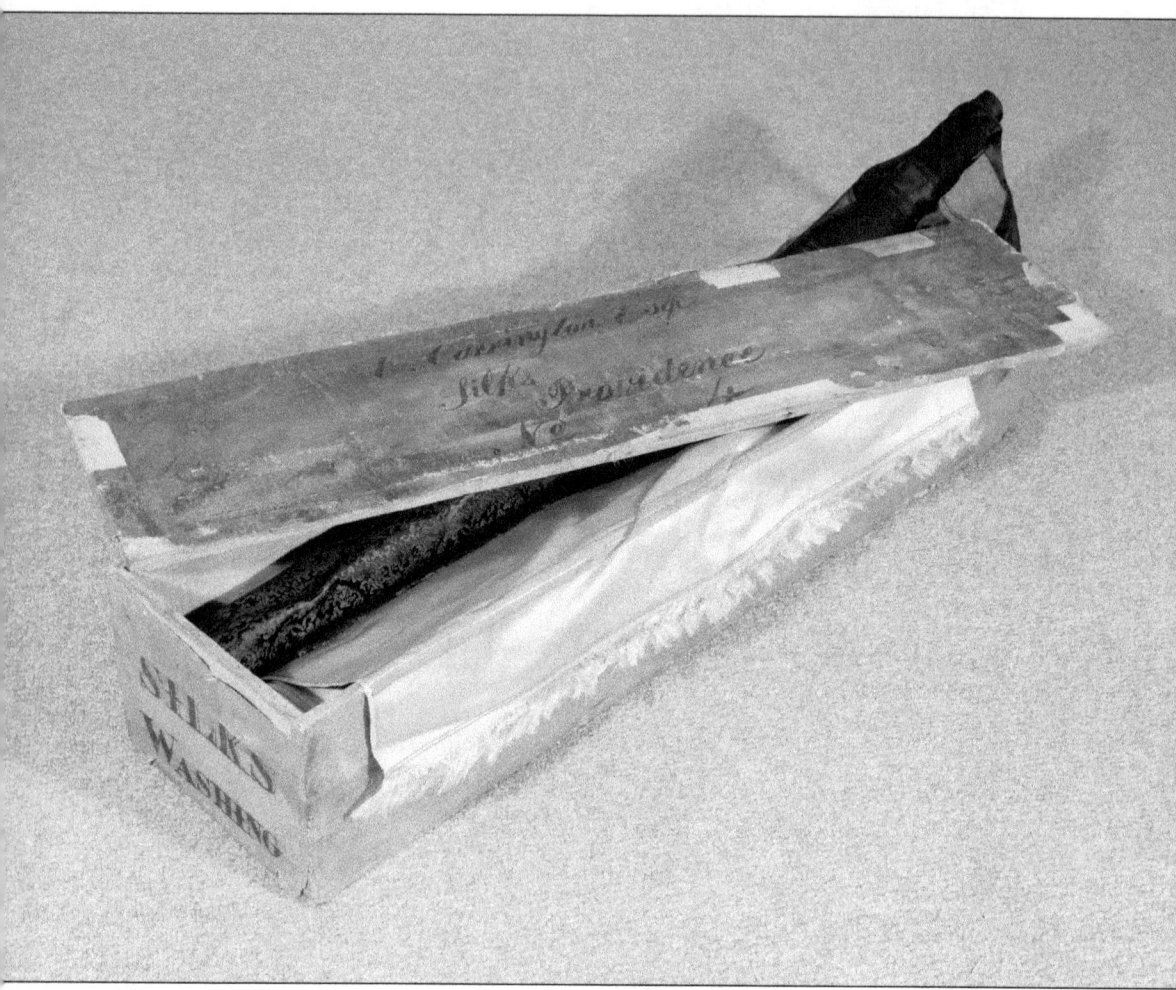

This image shows a packing box of silks contained in the collections of the Rhode Island Historical Society. The wooden shipping box is addressed to "E. Carrington Esq." and marked "Silk." Edward Carrington, Esq., was a successful shipping merchant in the early 19th century in Providence, gaining his wealth from his extensive dealings in the China trade. Rhode Islanders like Carrington and other prominent men of Providence like John Brown traded ginseng for silks, spices, teas, furniture, and porcelain, among other such goods from China. Ginseng was easily grown in the United States in places like Virginia and Pennsylvania, but it was more difficult to procure, though greatly sought-after, in China. Americans also traded Spanish bullion and sea otter pelts with the Chinese. The Carringtons lived at 66 Williams Street, half a block east of Benefit Street.

From a watercolor by W.L. Greene in 1898, this image is a composite of images depicting the Old Sabin House and the "Tyrannical Act of the *Britisher*." The event referenced by this image is the burning of the *Gaspee*, otherwise known as the Gaspee Affair, a precursor to the Boston Tea Party, during which Rhode Islanders violently demonstrated their frustration at British customs agents. On June 9, 1772, when John Brown's ship *Hannah* was being pursued by the customs vessel the *Gaspee* (with Lieutenant Dudingston presiding on board), the *Hannah* took the opportunity to lead the *Gaspee* onto a sandbar, where it became stuck. Learning of the stranded vessel, John Brown convened a group of men at Sabin's tavern to plot a violent takeover of the *Gaspee*, during which they rowed out in long boats, shot Dudingston, took him hostage, and burned the ship.

This portrait by J.C. Buttre, engraver, depicts Esek Hopkins (1718–1802), a merchant, and, most notably, commander-in-chief of the Continental Army during the American Revolution. Esek Hopkins has several ties to Benefit Street. Hopkins was employed by the four Brown brothers (John, Nicholas, Moses, and Joseph) to captain the *Sally* on an ill-fated voyage to Africa. Lasting from 1764 to 1765, the voyage saw the purchase of 196 slaves by Hopkins, the shipmaster; at least 109 of the Africans perished on the ship. In addition, Esek Hopkins's brother Stephen, governor of Rhode Island and a signer of the Declaration of Independence, lived in a modest red house that now resides on the corner of Benefit and Hopkins Streets. The Hopkins house has been moved twice, once to the other side of the street and another time up the hill using a system of ropes and pulleys. See page 86 for a photograph of the Stephen Hopkins House.

Edward Lee Peckham painted these images of the southern end of Benefit Street, part of an area known as Fox Point, in the 1830s. Fox Point, so named because the physical landscape resembled the head of a fox, was easily accessible to ships and thus was marked by numerous wharves. A year after this painting was complete, the Boston and Providence Railroad would construct its first station on the waterfront of Fox Point.

Substantial steamship trade began in the 1830s in the Narragansett Bay area. Its first commercial steamboat, the *Firefly*, arrived from New York and began to make regular trips between Providence and Newport. Well after steamboats were integrated in the New York and Long Island Sound areas, the steamer Robert Fulton traveled to Rhode Island from New York in 1821 and one year later, Narragansett Bay finally began to accept steamboats. Regular routes were formed between Providence and New York, and steamboat companies were at last established in Providence. From about 1836 to the start of World War II, steamboats were a dominant part of Narragansett Bay. It was the passage of the Steamboat Act of 1852 that made provisions for the appointment of steamboat inspectors by customhouse collectors. These steamboat inspectors were required to issue licenses following inspections as well as to enforce safety requirements.

This undated stereoview image shows one side of the Providence River, with one ship docked on the right, and part of a steamboat visible on left. Buildings along the waterfront are also visible on the right. Stereoview images were popular in the 19th century, as they gave the viewer the opportunity to trick the eye into seeing three-dimensional depth.

This 1882 image depicts the "college fruit vendor, Moke." The college referenced here is Brown University. Much of the selling and buying of wares on College Hill took place in Market Square, where Moke perhaps purchased the fruit that he sold to Brown University students. In 1927, a new produce center was opened on Harris Avenue, at which point the Market House and Market Square were no longer used for produce distribution. Additionally, if he were still selling produce in 1927, he would no longer be able to purchase his wares along the waterfront as the leases for spaces adjacent to the river were revoked.

This c. 1898 image depicts the Providence River, looking north. The spire of the Unitarian Church is visible, and a vendor sells Christmas trees on the waterfront. Margaret Bingham Stillwell, a writer who describes a childhood spent on Benefit Street, discusses the trend of walking downtown from Benefit Street to shop at the turn of the century. From the perspective of this photograph, the route down College Street and onto Westminster appears easily accessible.

This is Water Street, once referred to as the Towne Street. The Market House is visible in the lower left, to the right of which is an unpaved College Street. Horse-drawn carriages, waiting outside of businesses along Water Street, are also visible. (Photograph by Laurence Tilley.)

This c. 1930–1935 photograph shows a view of South Water Street looking south. A similar perspective is shown on page 42, yet this image was taken at least 30 years later. The most marked visible difference between the two images is the long line of cars, rather than horse-drawn carriages, parked outside of the waterfront businesses.

This sketch shows Fox Point, so named because the land seemed to form the shape of a fox's head. Various types of ships are presented in the sketch, underscoring the need for drawbridges along the Providence River, which would allow larger vessels to venture as far upstream as possible when engaged in trade.

This c. 1951 photograph was taken as part of Laurence Tilley's membership in the Camera Club of the Providence Engineering Society. The photograph shows South Water Street looking across Providence River toward the South Main Street area and seems to have been taken from a parking lot at the foot of Dorrance Street, facing east. (Photograph by Laurence Tilley.)

This 1840 view of India Point is a sketch of a painting by Kinsley C. Gadding. India Point was established as the first port of Providence in 1680, and a century later, it would continue to serve maritime interests, including those of prominent merchant John Brown. Brown participated heavily in the East Indies trade, bartering Spanish bullion and ginseng for teas, spices, porcelain, and other goods popular in the new nation. India Point was named for the heavy trading that went on in the Indies. In the early and mid-19th century, although maritime trade decreased from what it had been in John Brown's day, the development of railroad lines to India Point continued to support the prosperity of the India Point area.

This July 1920 photograph depicts several members of the chamber of commerce and various Providence port officials greeting officers of the S.S. *Providence*. The S.S. *Providence* was a steamship that was constructed for the Bristol Line but which soon after began to serve in the Fall River Line.

This 1880 photograph shows South Water and Dyer Streets. Several types of commerce are suggested by the image: two men sit to eat their lunch, possibly procured from a lunch wagon; barrels are loaded on wagons which will be taken to local businesses and sold; and cable cars transport paying customers to their destination.

This is an aerial view of the Crawford Street Bridge. In the lower right, a lunch cart is visible. Lunch carts and night lunch wagons (which stayed open until the early hours of the morning) offered inexpensive fare to first-, second-, and third-shift workers beginning in the late 19th century in Providence.

This 1867 image of the Providence River, looking south, depicts John P. Meriam and Company. John P. Meriam, who ran the wholesale fish store on the west side of the river, had his hand in another venture as well: he served on the board of directors at the State Bank and also served as its president for two decades.

This 1896 photograph shows the Providence River and the businesses along South Water Street. The spire of the First Baptist Church can be seen in the background. Similar in perspective to the second image on page 46, this photograph shows a change that has occurred in the flow of traffic near Market Square: a bridge has been added to allow easier access across the Providence River.

Four

"A LIBERAL EDUCATION"

The education offered in Providence in the late 19th century at institutions like the High School, shown here, had been dramatically changed since the early part of the century. The 1830s saw the establishment of Margaret Fuller's Greene Street School, which offered progressive education to young women and four decades later, a female candidate would apply for admission to Brown University. The candidate was denied admission, but her application spurred the creation of Pembroke College, a women's college at Brown.

Moses Brown, born on September 23, 1738, played an essential role in the history of Providence. He was a cofounder of Brown University as well as a strong abolitionist and industrialist. During the American Industrial Revolution, Brown funded the design and construction of some of the initial factories for spinning machines, including several at Slater Mill. Additionally, Moses was a member of the renowned Colonial shipping firm Nicholas Brown and Company, along with his three brothers, Nicholas, Joseph, and John. Among his siblings, he was the most politically active; as a representative from Providence, he served for eight years in the Rhode Island General Assembly. Brown's dedication to the antislavery movement made him a significant leader in not only Rhode Island but also New England. Brown was also a proponent of peace, inspired by the War of 1812, and was greatly involved in the founding of the Rhode Island Peace Society in 1818. Last but not least, Moses Brown was driven by his love for local history, and consequently, was a founding member of the Rhode Island Historical Society. He served for a time as its chairman and left the majority of his papers there after his death in 1836.

Judith Paul, a Providence resident, embroidered these words into her sampler work in 1791: "May spotless innocence and truth my every action guide and guard my unexperienced youth from arrogance and pride." The initial attempt to embroider a sampler was usually a simple one, with letters, numbers, the child's name, date, and perhaps some minimal decorative stitching. As students became more adept, the complexity and intricacy of the piece usually improved.

Betsey (Metcalf) Baker (1786–1867) was born in Providence, Rhode Island, to successful artisan Joel Metcalf. While the family lived on Benefit Street, Betsey kept a diary that chronicles how she taught herself, at the age of 12, to braid straw bonnets. Her craft brought her fame as the first American to master the English method, and she ran a successful business selling her bonnets. This oil-on-canvas portrait was painted in 1851 by James Sullivan Lincoln.

Providence constructed its first public high school at 205 Benefit Street, between Angell and Waterman Streets. The school was dedicated on March 20, 1843. Attendance at the school was initially restricted to white students. In 1865, however, the Rhode Island State Legislature mandated that students could not be denied admission based on race, and Maritcha Lyons became the first African American student to enroll in the school.

This c. 1900–1925 photograph shows Providence High School on the corner of Waterman and Benefit Streets. The state later purchased the school in 1877, transitioning it from a high school into a normal school. The building served other purposes as well in the late 19th and early 20th centuries: it housed the Rhode Island College of Pharmacy, the University School, and the Rhode Island Supreme Court. (Photograph by John Hess.)

This c. 1946 photograph shows a woman in the doorway of No. 44 and 42 Benefit Street, on the west side of the street. This house looks onto Jenckes Street, named after the Jenckes family, early settlers of Providence. Joseph Jenckes (1656–1740) served as governor of the colony of Rhode Island and Providence Plantations for five years. (Photograph by Charlotte Estey.)

William M. Williams was an 1889 graduate of Providence High School. The Providence with which Williams would have been familiar was a quickly expanding one: the India Point bridge was being replaced, the Public Park Association created Tockwotten Park in the Fox Point district, and Roger Williams Park was established for the entertainment of the public. Educational opportunities were expanding, too, as more and more schools were constructed for Providence's youth. During the decade leading up to William M. Williams's graduation from the Providence High School, 15 schoolhouses were built, including the Vineyard Street Grammar School.

The Providence High School is pictured here, this time in 1904. When the school, built in 1843, was enlarged into a normal school, a section was added to the rear of the building to allow for the inclusion of a laboratory space as well as other uses. This normal school was incorporated in 1871. The principal of the school was J.C. Greenough, and the board of education served the role of trustees of the school. John Hutchins Cady points out in the *Civic and Architectural Development of Providence* that the normal school was first opened in the Central Congregational Church before moving into its new location at 205 Benefit Street. (Photograph by John Hess.)

On February 8, 1876, a charter was granted to a group of 15 men by the State of Rhode Island to establish what was later named the Hope Club "for purposes of social and literary culture." After purchasing the property of Abraham Okie on Benevolent Street in 1885 and razing the existing house, the Hope Club financed what may have been the first building in the county erected for use as a clubhouse.

Five

A HAVEN FOR ARTISTS

The Providence Athenaeum at 251 Benefit Street is the fourth-oldest subscription library in the country. In 1753, a group of private citizens established the Providence Library Company with the goal of obtaining access to a collection of books that they could not individually afford. By paying a small subscription fee to the library, members could benefit from a larger, shared collection. At the time, many of the early books had to be purchased from England. Shortly after the College of Rhode Island moved to Providence in 1770, the library extended its services to students.

In 1922, the Providence Athenaeum was home to the "Scruples Shelf," which hid books by authors like D. H. Lawrence from impressionable patrons. The books were kept in a drawer known by the librarians as "the sewer." In 1971, the board of directors voted that the cache be "scrupulously and without fanfare desegregated and redistributed," to the dismay of two patrons who complained that all of the "best" books were now spread throughout the library and difficult to find.

The Gothic fountain outside the Providence Athenaeum was funded by Anna Richmond in 1873 so that pedestrians could pause for a refreshing drink after a climb up the hill. The words "Come here everyone that thirsteth" are carved into the granite structure. Legend has it that visitors who drink the water are "sure to return," but due to the age and condition of the fountain and its water source, drinking from it today is not recommended. As expressed by the Providence Athenaeum: "A drink may mean you'll never leave—except via ambulance—but feel free to enjoy the fountain's legendary past!"

John Russell Bartlett (1805–1886), born in Providence, left a commercial career in banking to pursue his passion for books, becoming a foreign book dealer in New York and, in 1836, a founder of the Providence Athenaeum on Benefit Street. Bartlett served for 17 years as secretary of the state for Rhode Island, during which time he worked to preserve for posterity the 17th-century records of Roger Williams.

One prominent member of the early library organization was Stephen Hopkins, a signatory of the Declaration of Independence. With the 1836 merger of the Providence Library Company and the Providence Athenaeum (founded in 1831 by Bartlett), the new organization became known as the Athenaeum. Two years later, a Greek Revival building was completed on Benefit Street in 1838. In 1850, an amendment to its charter altered the original name to the Providence Athenaeum; its interior is pictured below.

A two-story, granite Greek Revival structure with a recessed portico with two Doric columns, the Providence Athenaeum is the only New England building designed by prominent Philadelphia architect William Strickland. Two significant additions to the library occurred in 1914 and 1978, designed by local architect Norman Isham and award-winning architect Warren Platner, respectively.

The Providence Athenaeum is home to a variety of interesting collections, including classic novels, children's stories, paintings, and rare items, such as Joseph Brown's copy of James Gibbs's *Book of Architecture*.

Edgar Allan Poe visited Providence in 1845 to attend a lecture by his friend and poet, Frances Sargent Osgood. Poe had been in correspondence with Sarah Helen Whitman, a prominent female poet of the time, but had not yet met her. While leaning against an elm tree and enjoying an evening in the garden, Poe fell in love with Sarah as she picked roses in the moonlight behind her house on Benefit Street. The resulting courtship consisted of numerous rendezvous in the nearby Providence Athenaeum.

Sarah Helen Whitman was the fiancée of Edgar Allen Poe. She was also a genealogist and alleged that she and Edgar Allen Poe shared an Irish royal ancestry through the "Po'er" family. On December 23, 1848, at the Athenaeum, Sarah received a note questioning Poe's sobriety. Whitman immediately called off the wedding, left the Athenaeum, and returned to her house. She would never see Poe again.

An artist from New Brunswick, Canada, who settled in Rhode Island, Edward Mitchell Bannister (1828–1901) was known for his pastoral paintings. At the 1876 Philadelphia Centennial, Bannister won a bronze medal for his large oil painting, *Under the Oaks*. Bannister was part of a group of artists who founded the Providence Art Club, which resided in the Fleur-de-Lys building across the street from the First Baptist Church on Thomas Street. Bannister's wife, Christiana, is an equally interesting figure. Known as a "hair doctress," Christiana owned and operated a successful hair salon in Boston and then in Providence and was able to support her husband Edward's art through her business. Christiana Bannister spearheaded an initiative to open a space for retired African American women, the Home for Aged Colored Women. Bannister herself would be taken there for a brief period later in life.

Charles Loring Elliot (1812–1868) painted this c. 1845–1850 portrait of James Sullivan Lincoln. Apprenticed to the Providence portraitist C.T. Hinckley, Lincoln later became a celebrated portraitist in his own right, painting the likes of Ambrose Burnside, a Civil War general whose house still stands at 314 Benefit Street. In 1880, Lincoln was elected first president of the Providence Art Club.

Located at 11 Thomas Street, the Providence Art Club is considered to be the oldest art club in the United States after the Salmagundi Club of New York. A group of 16 men and women—all professional artists, amateurs, and art collectors—founded the club to inspire and encourage the love and appreciation of art in the Providence community. When the founders drew up their charter in February 1880, they inscribed their purpose on their seal: "For Art Culture." Quickly outgrowing their original quarters, in 1887 the club moved to its current clubhouse, the 1790 Obadiah Brown House. The Providence Art Club hosts gallery exhibitions, dramatic presentations, musical evenings, and lectures to further its mission of promoting and supporting the visual arts in Rhode Island.

John Holden Greene, famed Rhode Island architect, was born in Warwick in 1777 and died in Providence in 1850. Beginning in 1806 and ending in 1830, Greene successfully designed more than 50 buildings that were constructed in the city of Providence, many of which are still standing. On or near Benefit Street, Greene was responsible for the Sullivan Dorr House, John Larchar House, Truman Beckwith House, Benoni Cooke House, and the First Unitarian Church, all of which are still standing. Many of the buildings he designed were razed, including the Dexter Asylum, the Bristol Hotel, and several other buildings near Market Square.

A Richmond, Rhode Island, native, Thomas Alexander Tefft (1826–1859) was a nationally recognized architect, particularly famous for the Union Depot. Tefft designed the depot for the Providence & Worcester Railroad while a first-year student at Brown University. Tefft was also responsible for designing additions to the Nightingale-Brown House at 357 Benefit Street. The Nightingale-Brown House, now owned by Brown University, houses the John Nicholas Brown Center for Public Humanities and Cultural Heritage.

Susannah Paine (1792–1862) painted this portrait of Catherine Read Williams (1790–1872) sometime between 1825 and 1850. Catherine Williams, born in Providence, was a descendant of the Arnolds, a longstanding Rhode Island family. After an unhappy marriage that ended when she left her husband and took her infant daughter back to Rhode Island, Williams published a small volume of poems and launched a career as a writer, biographer, and local historian.

This 1867 photograph depicts Edward Lewis Peckham (1812–1889), the celebrated watercolorist. Peckham is well-known for his illustrations of Rhode Island wildflowers and other plants. The artist took care to mark the plant name, date, and location on each illustration.

This image shows the home of John Russell Bartlett at 225 Benefit Street. Bartlett, born in 1805 in Providence, Rhode Island, spent most of his childhood in Canada. When he was 22, he became a bookkeeper and head teller for several years at the Bank of North America & Providence, the bank of Cyrus Butler (Providence's wealthiest man at the time). In 1831, Bartlett founded the Providence Athenaeum, a library that would later merge with the Providence Library Company. Bartlett maintained a great love and appreciation for knowledge and books; he started Bartlett & Welford in New York, a publishing company that dealt with British and foreign books. Later returning to Providence, he served as the secretary of the state for Rhode Island from 1855 to 1872.

Matilda Sissieretta Joyner Jones (c. 1868–1933), known as Sissieretta Jones, was an African American soprano. Although born in Virginia, she grew up in Providence at Pratt and South Court Streets, one block east of Benefit Street. Jones, known as "the Black Patti," enjoyed much success touring and performing internationally and became the first African American woman to sing at Carnegie Hall.

Six
BENEFIT STREET IN WARTIME

This image is from the sheet music of "Burnside Zouaves March," published in 1868 and composed by the leader of the American Brass Band, David Wallis Reeves (1838–1900). The name "Zouaves" was co-opted by Americans during the Civil War to describe volunteer regiments donning the North African–inspired military ensemble of baggy trousers and sashes. After the war, Ambrose Burnside took up residence at 314 Benefit Street.

This 1892 painting by Charles Dewolf Brownell (1822–1909) depicts the burning of the *Gaspee* that occurred in June 1772. In the early morning hours, longboats filled with men frustrated by the trade limitations placed on them by the British Crown decided to take violent action by burning the ship and taking its captain, Lieutenant Dudingston, captive. The event has resonated strongly with Rhode Islanders ever since: the point off of which the Gaspee was burned was renamed Gaspee, and Warwick celebrates Gaspee Days to commemorate the event. George Washington celebrated the event himself in 1774 during a fireworks spectacle in Virginia, intended to mark the second anniversary of the burning. During the 19th century, Rhode Islanders began to mark the occasion with festivals and parades, which have continued into the 21st century.

This artifact, part of the collections at the Rhode Island Historical Society, is a wine goblet said to have been plundered from the *Gaspee* the night of June 9, 1772, when colonists set fire to the customs ship and took its captain, Lt. William Dudingston (1740–1817), hostage. Although Dudingston was not fatally wounded, he was shot in the groin and suffered considerable pain. John Mawney, a physician, tended to Dudingston wounds and performed surgery on him; Dudingston was later put to shore. After the Crown heard about the incident, a warrant was issued for the arrest of any persons connected to the case; John Brown, complicit in the affair, sent his family out of Providence for their safety. The date 1772 has been engraved on the goblet to tie the object to the event for perpetuity.

The Benefit Street Arsenal, also known as the State Arsenal, is located at 176 Benefit Street. Built in 1839, the arsenal was designed by James Bucklin, a Rhode Island architect who, along with Russell Warren, designed the Arcade on Westminster Street, the oldest standing arcade today. The arsenal was used as the armory of the Providence Marine Corps of Artillery and several associated artillery units in the Rhode Island Militia. During the Civil War, the armory was used as the mobilization site for 10 batteries of light artillery raised in Rhode Island. The arsenal was used by a variety of other organizations including the Grand Army of the Republic, the Sons of Union Veterans of the Civil War, and the United Spanish War Veterans. More recently, in 1970, the Benefit Street Arsenal was added to the National Register of Historic Places.

On May 17, 1924, the Benefit Street Arsenal was the site of an illegal meeting of the Ku Klux Klan. Although often associated with the South, the Klan was relatively active in Rhode Island during the 1920s. Klan members arranged a meeting at the State Arsenal that attracted about 200 men. The group had not obtained a permit to meet on state property but had gained access to the building by claiming it was hosting a religious meeting. Later, however, Rhode Island's governor William S. Flynn denounced the Klan and subsequently banned the group from using state property for meetings.

TO THE CITIZENS
OF PROVIDENCE!!!
You are reqested FORTHWITH to repair to the
State Arsenal and TAKE ARMS.
SAMUEL W. KING,
Governor of the State of Rhode Island.

Providence, May 17, 1842, 6 o'clock P. M.

This advertisement appeared in the *Providence Journal* in May 1842, in the midst of what would come to be called the Dorr Rebellion. A People's Convention, an organized group led by Thomas Wilson Dorr, drafted a new state constitution that granted suffrage for all white men after one year of residency in the state and regardless of whether or not they owned property. Individuals who supported Dorr's stance were referred to as Dorrites. Recent immigrants supported Dorr as he offered the opportunity for suffrage, whereas his opponent, Samuel Ward King, then governor of Rhode Island, did not. On May 19, 1842, the Dorrites launched an ultimately unsuccessful attack on the arsenal in Providence.

Robert Holloway was Ambrose Burnside's assistant and valet. After returning from the Civil War, Ambrose Burnside purchased a house at 314 Benefit Street. Holloway remained with Burnside for many years after the war, as well, dying in 1877. His epitaph reads: "30 years a faithful servant to Gen. Burnside, at Home and in the Field." (Photograph by Mathew Brady.)

This 1911 portrait shows James Newell Arnold (1844–1927), who published an extensive series of books detailing the vital records of Rhode Island towns, including birth, death, and marriage dates from 1636 to 1850. Arnold also documented cemeteries and burial grounds in the state, including the Tillinghast family burial ground on Benefit Street.

Civil War general Ambrose Burnside was famous for his unique hairstyle, which came to be known as "sideburns." Prior to the Civil War, Burnside was a prominent rifle manufacturer and owned the Burnside Rifle Company, one of the most respected arms manufacturers of the 1800s. When the war began, he severed ties with his rifle company so he could command the Rhode Island Volunteers. Although his military career was relatively unexceptional, he gained attention from growing his "sideboards" until they connected with his mustache. Later, the term changed from "sideboards" to "sideburns" in his honor. Post–Civil War, Burnside was known for his manufacturing and railroad endeavors; he was also a distinguished politician in Rhode Island.

At the outset of the Civil War, General Burnside organized the First Rhode Island Infantry, one of the first units to reach and protect the Washington capitol. At the battle of First Manassas, Burnside effectively directed an infantry brigade and was soon appointed to brigadier general of volunteers on August 6, 1861, followed by a promotion to major general of volunteers on March 18, 1862. However, his luck turned at the battle of Antietam when Burnside's overly precise orders led to confusion and delays, resulting in serious complications in capturing what is now referred to as Burnside's Bridge. Two major Union defeats, the Battle of Fredericksburg and the "Mud March," caused Burnside to be relieved of command. Despite brief success at Knoxville, another tragedy at Petersburg resulted in Burnside's resignation. After the war, Burnside became politically active, serving as governor of Rhode Island from 1866 to 1869 and as a Republican US senator from 1874 until his death in 1881.

Although the Civil War was not fought on Rhode Island soil, Rhode Islanders were active participants in the war effort. Back at home, wives and daughters participated in activities to raise funds for supplies and other necessities, including knitting groups and nursing wounded soldiers at hospitals like Portsmouth Grove in Portsmouth, Rhode Island. After the war was over, widows, disabled veterans, and their families needed additional assistance. In Providence, in the early 1860s, a group of five young women (teenagers) started the Irrepressible Society to help these individuals and to address what they called the "general charitable work of the city" of Providence. Mary Hoppin, pictured here, was one of the young women to take a leadership role in the Irrepressible Society.

Anne Ives Carrington, along with her friends Mary Hoppin (pictured above) and Candace Crawford Dorr Carrington (page 80), belonged to the Irrepressible Society. The group raised funds to purchase thread, fabric, and other materials and then constructed and distributed clothing to families in Providence. The group also distributed coal, shoes, and other provisions, depending on the needs of the family. The Irrepressible Society was divided into several committees, each responsible for a different part of the society's mission: the Visiting Committee, the Cutting Committee, and the Buying Committee. The Visiting Committee conducted visits with potential families to determine their needs and followed up with families who had received provisions and clothing from the society. The Cutting Committee was charged with cutting out the forms of clothing from the fabric, which had been purchased by the Buying Committee.

Like Anne Ives Carrington and Mary Hoppin, Candace Crawford Dorr Carrington grew up near Benefit Street and joined her friends in operating the Irrepressible Society, a charitable organization in Providence. To raise funds, the Irrepressible Society put on theatricals at some of the local theaters. These events were advertised in the *Providence Journal* and were extremely successful. The society raised enough money to begin paying some members of low-income families to cut and sew clothes that would be distributed to other families. According to the records kept by the Irrepressible Society, the organization continued to grow each year, increasing the number of programs it undertook and reaching more families in Providence. The valentine pictured here, part of the Carrington Collection at the Rhode Island Historical Society, would have been created by young women like Candace and disseminated to her friends who lived along Benefit Street and in the surrounding neighborhood.

Benefit Street saw its share of spectacles, both in wartime and peacetime. Funeral processions used Benefit Street, and Theodore Roosevelt paraded down the street during a visit to Providence in 1902. During the 1886 sesquicentennial of Rhode Island's founding as well as the 1936 tercentenary, Providence citizens paraded through the streets of the city, including Benefit Street. Newspapers like the *Providence Journal* remarked on the elaborate decorations and splendor adorning houses and businesses, pictured here at a World War I victory celebration at Exchange Place on May 5, 1919.

Helen Clarke Grimes (1905–1989) left several diaries that chronicle her life in Rhode Island during World War II. In 1942, she describes coming into Providence with her husband Dorrance, parking at the Rhode Island School of Design, and walking up to Prospect Terrace to see the city at night. Grimes writes that though she never loved Providence, she is "very fond" of the East Side and really [loves] Prospect Terrace. "It is the only small park in the city where one can sit and dream without feeling like a loafer or a tired street-walker."

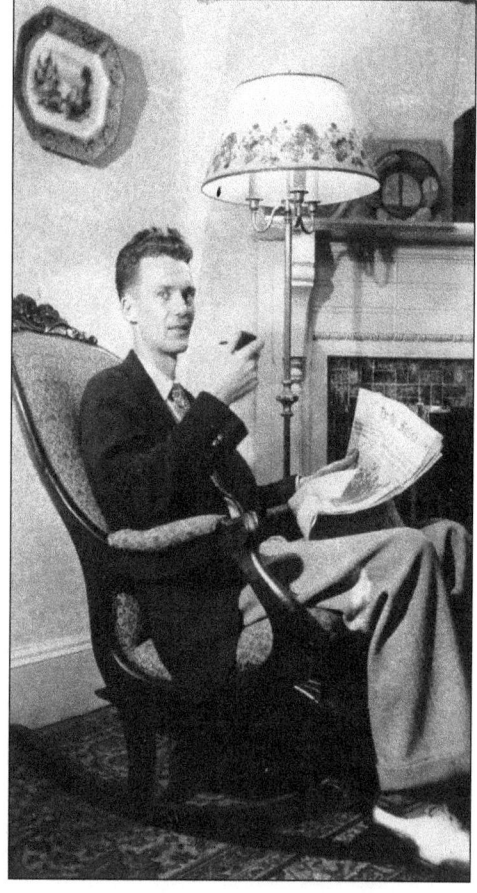

Seven
TAKING A STAND

From 1681 until 1854, Rhode Island government rotated among the state's five counties. Each of the five counties had its own seat of government and state house, where the executive, legislative, and judicial branches would meet. However, in 1854, the rotation was divided solely between Newport and Providence until 1901, at which point Providence was named the only capital of Rhode Island. The current seat of state government, the Rhode Island State House, was completed in Providence in that same year.

The General Assembly rotated meetings in different towns in the state including Providence and Newport until the middle of the 19th century. The brick Georgian-style exterior of the Old State House, pictured here, was modeled after the Newport Colony House. In addition to being the site of Rhode Island's 1776 Declaration of Independence, George Washington visited a second time in 1790 to celebrate Rhode Island's ratification of the US Constitution, which made it the last of the 13 colonies to join the Union.

The Old State House, listed in the National Register of Historic Places in 1970, is also part of the College Hill Historic Landmark District, so designated in 1971. The commanding building projects the stateliness required by such an important seat of government. This brick and brownstone building that once housed the colony's government offices as well as the government library is now occupied by the Rhode Island Historical Preservation and Heritage Commission.

Architecturally, the Old State House is representative of the late English Baroque of the William and Mary and Queen Anne period. Its symmetrical composition and utilization of red brick with rusticated brownstone and painted wood trim are its defining characteristics. During the time of the American Revolution in the late 1700s, this building was the site of powerful debates between parties represented by John and Moses Brown regarding slavery, particularly the proposal by some slaveholders to free their slaves so that they could serve as soldiers.

Stephen Hopkins has been called Rhode Island's "greatest statesman." He was one of the two Rhode Islanders to sign the Declaration of Independence. Suffering from palsy in his hands in 1776, he signed the document while holding his right hand with his left, saying, "[M]y hand trembles, but my heart does not." In 1743, Hopkins purchased a home that had been built in 1708. He made a substantial, two-story addition to the original structure, including a single ground-floor room on either side of a central hallway and two chimneys. George Washington is said to have visited Hopkins in his home. Today, Hopkins's possessions can be viewed by visitors, including two Queen Anne chairs, his silver porringer, shoe buckles, a baby bonnet, and shoes. The Stephens Hopkins House is currently overseen by the National Society of the Colonial Dames of America.

Stephen Hopkins (1707–1785), 10 times the governor of Rhode Island (alternating with his opponent Samuel Ward King), was a chief justice on the Rhode Island Supreme Court and one of two Rhode Islanders (along with William Ellery Channing of Newport) to sign the Declaration of Independence. Hopkins later held a seat in the First Continental Congress as one of Rhode Island's two delegates from 1774 to 1780. Hopkins's modest red house was moved up the hill to Benefit Street in 1927 to make room for the construction of a new courthouse.

George Washington visited Providence in 1790, immediately after Rhode Island made the decision to ratify the Constitution, the very last state to agree to do so. This copy of Charles Willson Peale's portrait of Washington was owned by John Brown, a fervent admirer and staunch supporter of the general who anxiously awaited the ratification of the Constitution to encourage the president's visit. In fact, John Brown was such a fan of Washington that he named three of his ships after him. The portrait, along with Charles Willson Peale's portrait of Martha Washington, hangs in the John Brown House Museum at 52 Power Street.

During George Washington's visit to Providence in 1790, he stayed at the Golden Ball Inn, later called the Mansion House, at 81 Benefit Street. While staying at the inn, Washington purportedly took an evening stroll up the hill to see University Hall illuminated with candles in each window. Washington and his entourage met with several important political figures in the town of Providence, including John Brown, who invited the general to visit his newly constructed house at 52 Power Street. Washington rode in John Brown's carriage, which has been carefully restored and resides at the John Brown House Museum.

This undated image shows an 18th-century residence along Benefit Street, likely on the Southern end. Benefit Street South was home to many Cape Verdean families who came to Providence in the 19th and 20th centuries. In the early 1800s, many Cape Verdean immigrants participated in the whaling industry. In the 20th century, Cape Verdeans responded to the call for workers in Providence's textile industry.

Eight
BENEFIT STREET SOUTH

This c. 1950 photograph depicts three boys and a bicycle, possibly along South Main Street. The boy in the cowboy hat is named Raymond Johnson. Born in Westerly, Rhode Island, Charlotte Estey, a photojournalist, documented many such scenes around Providence during the first part of the 20th century. (Photograph by Charlotte Estey.)

Now known as the Old Stone Bank, the Providence Institution for Savings was founded in 1819 as a mutual savings bank. Located currently at 86 South Main Street, the bank was first located at 43 South Main Street. The original three-story structure, owned by Peter Grinnell & Son, was destroyed by fire in 1837. According to one of the bank's cash journals now contained within the Rhode Island Historical Society's collections, "all the office furniture, together with a great quantity of books and documents were consumed" in the fire. A landmark on South Main Street, the Old Stone Bank structure is noted for its roof featuring a gold-leaf dome.

These photographs depict the remodeling that occurred at the Old Stone Bank in 1898. The first photograph shows the teller windows with one of the large, half-circle exterior windows visible at the top. The second photograph shows the end of a line of teller windows and an entrance to an office at the right. Founded in 1819 as the Providence Institution for Savings, the mascot of the Old Stone Bank eventually became Fred Flintstone. In advertisements for the bank, Fred Flintstone would exclaim, "Yabba-dabba-doo, love that Old Stone Bank!" Continuing with the theme put forth by their mascot, the ATM machines at the bank were called "Ready Freddy."

The undated photograph above shows South Main Street looking south. To the left of the Old Stone Bank, 50 South Main Street was the home of Joseph Brown, architect, astronomer, and one of the four prominent Brown brothers. Across the street from 50 South Main stood John Brown's townhouse that he left in order to build his brick mansion at 52 Power Street.

This early 20th-century photograph depicts the owner of a European tobacco store, possibly located on South Main Street. Tobacco stores like the one on South Main Street were common in the 19th century well as the 20th.

The photograph to the right shows the same European tobacco store (and its owner) on page 94. The photograph below shows several men standing on the sidewalk on Wickenden Street during the early or mid-20th century. Wickenden Street, part of Fox Point, was named after the British minister William Wickenden, who owned a farm that was located on the site where the street is now located. Beginning in the 19th century, the Wickenden Street area has welcomed many Irish, Portuguese, and Cape Verdean immigrants.

This c. 1950 photograph shows a young girl in a white print dress, socks, and shoes, holding her doll next to the curb. The photograph was likely taken in the Fox Point neighborhood. (Photograph by Charlotte Estey.)

Immigrants coming to Providence faced many obstacles, particularly those who spoke a foreign language or were of a lower economic status, like many of the families who came to settle in the southern part of Benefit Street. The Italian Americans in this 1903 image are shown at the refuse dump on Westminster Street.

These Italian Americans are sifting through materials at the refuse dump on Westminster Street in 1903.

This c. 1950 photograph shows Bea, Mendes, and Lopez on an unknown ship. During the 19th and 20th centuries, packet ships, largely run by Cape Verdeans, provided transportation and the conveyance of commercial goods to and from Cape Verde. (Photograph by Charlotte Estey.)

Immigrants aboard the *Venezia* arrive at the new Providence State Pier on opening day, December 17, 1913.

This c. 1950 photograph highlights a man playing guitar, probably in South Main Street or the Fox Point area. (Photograph by Charlotte Estey.)

This c. 1950 photograph shows 42 and 44 Wickenden Street. The image highlights a gentleman with his hands in his pocket, identified as Joe "Ball." (Photograph by Charlotte Estey.)

This 1835 photograph shows the Boston & Providence railroad carriage. The Boston & Providence line was extended in the 1830s, and the first station was constructed on Fox Point in 1835.

This 1930 image shows buildings along North Main Street. Note a large sign that reads "National Wiper and Supply."

This waterfront pass was issued to Gustaf Swanson on May 3, 1918. According to the record, Swanson worked as a teamster for the American Screw Company. Formed in 1860, the American Screw Company manufactured wood and machine screws as well as rivets. The Waterfront Pass was necessary in 1918 while the United States was at war to regulate exactly who was allowed to be near the docks.

This painting, attributed to Edward Lewis Peckham (1812–1889), was completed in 1839; it shows a length of Benefit Street looking south with a view of the Providence River.

This photograph captures the scene at the corner of Williams and South Main Streets.

This c. 1951 image shows the building at 320 South Main Street. The exterior facade of the building is painted with an advertisement touting the merits of the "Famous Narragansett Ale Lager Friendly Bar." (Photograph by Charlotte Estey.)

This c. 1951 image shows a building located at 312 South Main Street. It was owned by Rebekah and Peleg Williams, built c. 1770. (Photograph by Charlotte Estey.)

This c. 1951 image depicts 275 South Main Street, which, at this time, housed Goldberg's Furniture Store. (Photograph by Charlotte Estey.)

This c. 1951 image shows buildings at 254 and 256 South Main Street. The sign for the store on the right reads "Tools We Buy." (Photograph by Charlotte Estey.)

This c. 1951 image shows "Minna Andrade" in her confirmation dress. Minna is standing at 36 Wickenden Street. (Photograph by Charlotte Estey.)

This 1903 photograph shows a view along North Main Street. Children are playing outside of the Providence remnants store located at 351 North Main Street.

Employees of the company Brown and Sharpe are pictured along South Water Street in 1872. Brown and Sharpe were developers of machine tools and machining technology, including tool making, measurement, and production.

105

This c. 1950 image features Phyllis Fortes Arajuo and Bonnie Gonsalves. (Photograph by Charlotte Estey.)

This c. 1951 photograph shows the intersection of South Main Street and Wickenden Street. (Photograph by Charlotte Estey.)

This c. 1951 photograph shows a building at 404 South Main Street. (Photograph by Charlotte Estey.)

Nine
MILE OF HISTORY, MILE OF MEMORIES

This is a rear view of the Shepley Library at 292 Benefit Street. Margaret Stillwell, a local historian who grew up on Benefit Street at the turn of the 20th century, recalls that just beyond the John Brown House stood a "little building put up by Colonel George Shepley to house his collection of Rhode Island books, prints, and manuscripts."

This compass, which dates to the early 17th century, was used by Roger Williams on his trek across Massachusetts in 1636. The compass boasts a screw top, is finely engraved, and has a folding sun-vane. It was donated to the Rhode Island Historical Society in 1902 by Sophia Augusta Brown, the widow of John Carter Brown, who had died in 1874. John Carter Brown's extensive library and a building fund were bequeathed to Brown University, and the John Carter Brown Library was constructed two blocks east of Benefit Street and dedicated in 1904. Sophia was a collector in her own right, amassing a manuscript collection that included Shakespeare folios and illuminated church manuscripts.

Transit Street got its name from the phenomenon of the "transit" of the planet Venus directly between the sun and Earth. It was observed on a June morning in 1769 by Joseph Brown, Moses Brown, Jabez Bowen, and Stephen Hopkins through a telescope that was set up 100 feet east of the northeast corner of Benefit and Transit Streets. The transits of Venus occur in pairs about eight years apart. This phenomenon occurred in 1761 and 1769, 1874 and 1882, 2004 and 2012, and is predicted for years 2117 and 2225.

The Sullivan Dorr House at 109 Benefit Street was designed in 1810 by architect John Holden Greene. Dorr pursued the fur trade, leaving the United States when he was 20 years old, and became a shipping magnate involved in the China trade. In addition to serving as a Brown University trustee and the second president of the Providence Washington Insurance Company, Dorr was the father of Thomas Wilson Dorr, the governor who led Dorr's Rebellion in 1842. Sullivan Dorr died on March 3, 1858, and was buried at the Swan Point Cemetery in Providence.

The Old State House (pictured below, second building from the left) was constructed in 1762. Known at various times throughout history as the Providence Colony, Providence County, Providence Court, or State House, the building assumed the popular name Old State House in 1901, after the new capitol on Smith Hill was occupied. In this building on May 4, 1776, the General Assembly repealed its act of allegiance to the British Crown; the date is now celebrated as Rhode Island Independence Day. Then in 1781, George Washington appeared at a dinner and ball given here in his honor. In 1784, it was in the Old State House that the assembly passed the first act in the nation providing for the gradual emancipation of slaves. The image above shows Benefit Street looking north from the Old State House.

In April 1899, discussions about opening a club for "literary, scientific, artistic and social purposes" were held between Prof. Edmund Burke Delabarre and Frederick T. Guild, registrar at Brown University. After recruiting several others for the project, the group secured the Rufus Waterman estate, situated on the corner of Benefit and Waterman Streets in August 1899. The University Club opened officially on December 29, 1899. The club, situated at 219 Benefit Street, is the building on the far left in the image below.

Prior to 1700, Providence townspeople buried their dead in family plots on their own individual properties. However, near the turn of the century, a combination of population growth and increasing property values led to the establishment of a common burying place that was outside prime building areas. The image at right shows one such burying ground, between Benefit Street and South Main Street, that was moved to make way for residential properties.

Howard Phillips Lovecraft, the famous author of "weird fiction," was born on August 20, 1890, at his family home at 454 (at the time, 194) Angell Street in Providence. Lovecraft was an intelligent boy: he could recite poetry at age two, read at age three, and began writing at age six or seven. Following the death of his father and grandfather and a move from his childhood birthplace, Lovecraft became reclusive from 1908 to 1913. After a failed marriage to Sonia Greene, Lovecraft moved back to Providence in April 1926 to 10 Barnes Street, north of Brown University, where he lived until May 1933. It is here that he wrote *The Dunwich Horror* and *The Call of Cthulhu*. He lived at his final address, 66 College Street, behind the John Hay Library, until he died in March 1937. Lovecraft was buried at the Phillips family plot at Swan Point Cemetery.

The John Larchar House at 282 Benefit Street was designed by John Holden Greene, the famed Providence architect. Built between 1818 and 1820, the large brick house was designed in the Federal style by John Holden Greene and is located adjacent to the First Unitarian Church. The cupola on the roof was not original to the house but was constructed as a later addition in the 19th century, along with the garage.

The Mansion House hosted prestigious clientele during the late 18th and early 19th centuries. When Benefit Street was still called Back Street, many prominent receptions and balls were held in its hall. In May 1790, when the Mansion House was known as the Golden Ball Tavern, Pres. George Washington was a guest here. Pres. John Adams and his family also stayed at the Mansion House while traveling to Massachusetts in 1797. The building was demolished in 1941. The building pictured below, adjacent to the Mansion House on Benefit Street, was also demolished.

This photograph documents the fifth anniversary banquet of Rev. M. Jerome Brown (1909–1979) on October 19, 1953. It forms part of the Congdon Street Baptist Church collection at the Rhode Island Historical Society. Reverend Brown ministered for 10 years at the Congdon Street Baptist Church, overseeing the start the Flower Group and the Lend-A-Hand auxiliary groups.

This view of South Water Street looking south is dated to August 1904. The image shows several old warehouses lining the street facing the Providence River. Also on view is the building that houses the Smith and Holden Company that sold shellac and gasoline in the early 20th century.

The abode of Thomas F. Hoppin, at 383 Benefit Street, was known as the "House of 1,000 Candles" since it served as the central location of Providence's social and cultural life, hosting receptions, banquets, musicals, and balls. Designed by architect Alpheus C. Morse, the refined, brick and brownstone mansion was one of the largest homes in Providence at the time. It was built on the lot of the 1791 John Innis Clarke House that was destroyed in a fire in 1849. Anna Almy Jenkins, granddaughter of Moses Brown, and her daughter Eliza Almy died in the fire. In 1838, Anna and Elizabeth were responsible for founding a charitable organization called the Providence Shelter for Colored Children.

Designated a National Historic Landmark in 1970, the Thomas P. Ives House is a three-story brick building erected between 1803 and 1805. It is similar in size to the John Brown House. In 1796, Thomas P. Ives and Nicholas Brown created a business enterprise, Brown and Ives, and engaged in trade with the Far East and Europe.

John Hutchins Cady (1881–1960), the noted architect and architectural historian, took this photograph of Power Street from South Main Street sometime between 1940 and 1950. Cady documented the early history of Providence in the seminal text *Civic and Architectural Development of Providence* as well as smaller pamphlets like *Highroads and Byroads of Providence* that detail the important thoroughfares of the city, including Benefit Street.

This c. 1900–1905 photograph shows the Donovan Brothers storefront at 313 North Main Street. The reverse of the photograph identifies the following subjects from left to right: Patrick Donovan, Dick McGuin, unidentified, Joseph Donovan, Gerald Donovan, and Mrs. Welch (in the second floor window). The Donovan Brothers boasted of selling "all the best brands of soap at wholesale" as well as eggs, butter, cheese, lard, pure spices, other sundries, and groceries.

The photograph above shows South Main Street looking north from Planet Street in April 1951. It was taken as part of the Camera Club of the Providence Engineering Society. The photograph below shows the Providence Boy's Club Building located at 226 South Main Street on the corner of Power Street. The Providence Engineering Society was founded in 1789, and its headquarters was 195 Angell Street during the time that J.M. Latham took these photographs. This building contained a darkroom that was used by the auxiliary Camera Club to which Latham belonged. (Photographs by J.M. Latham.)

This 1903 photograph shows an area of South Water Street that was known as "Cotton Row." Providence possesses a long history with cotton textile production. In 1790, Moses Brown, who had previously studied the process of cotton yarn production with little success, funded Samuel Slater's reworking of his machines and thus the factory-based system of production was born.

This photograph of South Main Street looks north from Planet Street, which takes its name from the transit of Venus. (Photograph by J.M. Latham.)

On January 3, 1899, at 283 Benefit Street, Harrielle S. Watson married John B. Lewis. This photograph, taken on their wedding day, represents the Victorian style of furnishing that would have been reflected in many of the homes on Benefit Street, including 34 Benefit Street (in the photograph below) and the John Brown House. From 1854 to 1901, the John Brown House was owned by the Gammell family. Elizabeth Gammell, a descendant of John Brown's daughter Sarah "Sally" Brown Herreshoff, decorated the house in the high Victorian style, including velvet drapes and a staircase with glass steps.

Robert Ives Gammell, son of Elizabeth Ives and Prof. William Gammell, entered the firm of Brown and Ives in 1874. He also assumed the major responsibility of handling his grandfather Robert Ives's vast estate, particularly upon his mother's death. Previously the director, Gammell succeeded his uncle William Goddard as president of Providence Bank in 1905, remaining in that position until his death in 1915. Robert Gammell also served on the boards of the Rhode Island Hospital Trust Company and the Providence Institution for Savings, as well as being treasurer of Blackstone Manufacturing Company.

Sarah Helen Power Whitman, born in 1803, was a renowned Providence poet. A life-long resident of Providence, she has been considered one of the "best female poets of America." She was widely read; in one of her essays alone, she cites 33 authors and three current periodicals. Moreover, Whitman was fluent in German, French, and Italian. Following the death of her husband, John Winslow Whitman, in 1833, her writing gained increased critical attention. She also became actively engaged in feminism and spiritualism, two movements that became extremely popular in the mid-19th century. Most of her essays were composed after 1850, and many of them were published in the *Providence Daily Journal*.

Both photographs, by the journalist John Hess, are part of his extension collection housed at the Rhode Island Historical Society. The 1906 image above shows the Eliza Ward House on the corner of George and Benefit Streets. The image below, undated, shows the front of the Shepley Library at 292 Benefit Street (Photographs by John Hess.)

In 1904, Julia Lippitt Mauran, Mary Parsons, and eight other women, all crafts enthusiasts, founded the Handicraft Club in Providence. Their mission was to stimulate interest in all kinds of handicrafts and to provide a setting to foster creativity. A variety of classes were offered, including bookbinding, silver and metal work, woodcarving, enameling, pottery, basketry, jewelry making, weaving, and photography. In 1925, the Handicraft Club had enough funds to purchase the Truman Beckwith House on College Hill, its present site.

Thomas Street, pictured here, looking east toward 195 Benefit Street, is lined with studios, galleries, and the Providence Art Club. 195 Benefit Street was built in 1879, but the site was home to Fanny Staples's school for children in 1870.

The Rhode Island School of Design, located at the base of College Hill, was founded by women in 1877 and its original library in the building, pictured here, was founded in 1878. In 2006, the library was moved to the former Rhode Island Hospital Trust Bank. The RISD Library is one of the oldest independent art college libraries in the country and has more than 150,000 volumes in circulation on subjects such as art, photography, architecture, and design. The towers at the top right, which belonged to the Central Congregational Church (now RISD's Memorial Hall) were damaged in the hurricane of 1938.

In 1827, Truman Beckwith, seeking seclusion from the other residential areas, chose to locate his Colonial-style brick mansion up the steep grade of College Hill. Designed by John Holden Greene, it was purchased in 1925 by the Handicraft Club, whose preservation efforts resulted in recognition from the Rhode Island Historical Preservation & Heritage Commission.

This image depicts the Robert H. Ives Gammell House, formerly at the northwest corner of the John Brown House lawn, at the corner of Benefit and Charlesfield Streets. In 1878, following his marriage to Elisa Anthony Hoppin, he and his growing family moved into his grandfather Robert Ives's former house, located at 327 Benefit Street adjacent to his parents' home.

This undated photograph shows Benefit Street at the corner of Thomas Street as it looked before being paved. Despite the many residences that line the street, the photograph is a reminder that Benefit Street was once part of a ridge in a hill that ultimately was carved out "for the common benefit of all."

Visit us at
arcadiapublishing.com

www.ingramcontent.com/pod-product-compliance
Lightning Source LLC
Chambersburg PA
CBHW050541110426
42813CB00008B/2226